THiS BOOK
BELONGS TO

....

....

WHAT'S IN A NAME

EXERCISE:

Have you ever Googled yourself before? Or at the very least the meaning of your name? No time like the present right? Open your search engine and find out what your name means.
Found it? Draw the meaning of your name.

WHY:

In mythology and fairytales names hold a lot of power. Think of Rumplestiltskin who's whole scheme got foiled by a simple soldier who discovered his one true name.

There are also certain names that immediately make you think of a certain type of person. Think of a 'Karen'.

While you are doing this exercise think of the power your name holds over you? Does the meaning suit you? Or do you think another name would be a better fit?

NAME:
MEANING:

THE PERFECT GIFT

EXERCISE:

Christmas is usually the happiest time of the year, but this time is extra special because you get to be the Grinch. Put some Christmas presents under the tree of someone you can't stand.

WHY:

This is a perfect way for you to get some more insight into who has the most power over you: the little devil or the little angel on your shoulder.

Will you be the bigger person and make everybody's Christmas wonderful with some fabulous gifts? Or will you choose evil and stick them with a lump of choal? Let's find out.

IF I WeRe YOU...

EXERCiSe:

You know yourself better than anyone else right? So how would you handle the situation if you were your own therapist?

Imagine sitting across from yourself on a comfortable chair while you are pouring your heart out. What is your diagnosis and your recommended course of action?

WHY:

We are often very good at offering advice to anybody but ourselves. For this exercise, it is important to step outside of yourself.

With this exercise, you are encouraged to look at your current situation from another perspective. This may shed a whole different light on your situation or your state of mind. It may even reveal solutions to problems that seemed insurmountable before.

Therapy notes

MY LiFe iN ReCeiPTS

EXeRCiSe:

Go through your wallet, your pockets, and your bags, and collect all the receipts that are in their. Write a story based on the purchases you've made over the last couple of days that is completely unrelated to the truth.

WHY:

People often think that creativity is inspired by beautiful dreams, wonderful visions, or big ambitions. This exercise will show you that even the most mundane things that inspire totally unique stories and fantasies.

FORTUNE COOKIES

EXERCISE:

Don't you just love fortune cookies. It's always a thrill when you get one that feels like it was made just for you. Let's make some for your loved ones. Fill the papers on the next page with fortunes for the people in your life.

WHY:

This exercise is a good way to practice your empathic skills. Instead of thinking of your own hopes and dreams think about what would make your loved ones happy.

Try seeing things from their perspective. Think of their successes and their struggles and give them a fortune that will make their future even brighter.

FiRST CRUSH

EXERCiSE:

Do you remember your first crush? What was it about that person that made you feel butterflies in your stomach? Was it the way they treated you? Was it something about the way they looked? Was it their sense of humor?

WHY:

Your first crush says a lot about you as a person. So when you want to get to know yourself better it is good to reflect on this special person in your life. Also note the differences between your first crush and your current crush.

M.A.S.H.

EXERCISE:

Play a game of M.A.S.H. on this page. M.A.S.H. is a fun future-telling game. The abbreviation stands for Mansion, Apartment, Shack, and House.

Write down 5 options for each of the categories on the following page. Next: you draw a spiral and stop at a random moment. Count the gaps between the spiral and start counting your options starting with the M. for M.A.S.H. cross out the option you land on when you reach the magic number and repeat until you only have one option left in each category.

What does your future have in store for you?

WHY:

For one thing, it's simply a fun thing to do. It's also a great way to help you imagine a crazy future without any risk of becoming overwhelmed by expectations, hopes and dreams. This is just for fun!

the magic number is 6

M.A.S.H.

WIFE: **# OF KIDS:**

JOB: **SALARY:**

VEHICLE: **PET:**

RESULT:

MUSIC AND LYRICS

EXERCISE:

Write or draw something inspired by a lyric from a song. If you have trouble choosing a song just put your playlist on shuffle and use the first song that comes up.

WHY:

Music is made to inspire emotions. This exercise will challenge you to listen mindfully to the lyrics of a song. What happens to you when you focus so completely on the lyrics?

Some people see a whole movie trailer in their mind when they listen to music. For others, it can trigger certain memories. What do you see? What does it make you feel?

Think about that and let your creativity flow freely!

NONE OF YOUR BUSINESS

EXERCISE:

If you had to start your very own business today what would it be? Make a business plan for a crazy, over-the-top company and design a logo to match.

WHY:

Thinking about starting a business is a great way to not only practice creativity but also your problem solving skills.

It requires you to anticipate obstacles that you may face and forces you to come up with ways to overcome those obstacles.

In order to start a successful business you need to be able to view a situation from a multitude of angles.

NaMe YOUR BUSINESS:

WHaT'S YOUR BUSINESS aLL aBOUT:

MY LOGO:

ROLE PLAY

EXERCISE:

Role-playing games aren't just for computers and bedrooms. They are popular in all sorts of shapes and sizes. And why wouldn't they be. It's fun to pretend to be someone else for a little while. Design your own RPG-character on the next page.

WHY:

Playing pretend makes it sound more childish than it actually is, but it is accurate. Pretending to be someone else can be a great way to step back from problems in your personal or professional life.

It's also very empowering to play a warrior elf with the ability to rapid fire flaming arrows at your enemy or to pretend you are a witch or warlock that has the power to cast spells on your adversaries.

CHARACTER

Name:	Portrait:

Appearance:

Personality:

Strength:	0 ○ ○ ○ ○ ○ ○ ○ ○ ○ ○	10
Kindness:	0 ○ ○ ○ ○ ○ ○ ○ ○ ○ ○	10
Charm:	0 ○ ○ ○ ○ ○ ○ ○ ○ ○ ○	10
Intellect:	0 ○ ○ ○ ○ ○ ○ ○ ○ ○ ○	10
Magical ability:	0 ○ ○ ○ ○ ○ ○ ○ ○ ○ ○	10

What does your character do in the story?

Quirks :	Notes:

CHEER FOR YOURSELF

EXERCISE:

It's time to boost your self-esteem a bit. And who better to hype you up than yourself? For this exercise we dare you to be your own personal cheerleader and write a cheer for yourself. You can repeat it whenever you need to be hyped up.

WHY:

Everybody has that little voice in the back of their head, but something that not everybody knows is that that voice can be a bully from time to time.

The only way to combat the negativity your inner voice will have you believe about yourself is by practicing positive self-talk.

VROOM VROOM

EXERCISE:

There are many ways to get from A to B, but none of them are particularly fun. Come up with an original and fun mode of transportation.

WHY:

Once upon a time we had to walk everywhere, until someone saddled a horse. It sounds like such a small thing, but it has made a big difference in the world.

This challenge will help you practice your creative problem-solving skills as well as your imagination. I wonder what form of transportation you come up with to get from A to B.

One thing though: try not to be boring by saying 'transportation'.

IN THE CLOUD

EXERCISE:

We are very dependent on the cloud nowadays, but do you ever take the time to study the actual clouds outside? Go outside, lay down on the ground and look at the clouds floating by. Try to find ones that resemble something and draw them on the next page.

WHY:

I think that everybody at one point has laid down on the grass to stare up at the clouds. They are kind of like a giant inkblot test in the sky if you think about it.

What do you see in the clouds that are floating by today? A rabbit, a butterfly, a skillet.

What do you think it says about you?

CaRTOONiFY YOURSeLF

EXERCiSe:

Have you ever really studied your face? Stand in front of the mirror and really look at yourself. Write or draw a caricature of yourself on the next page. Be sure to really accentuate your most noticeable features and be kind to yourself.

WHY:

Have you ever felt uncomfortable staring at your own reflection? Too bad, because a big part of creativity is being comfortable with yourself. Besides, everybody is beautiful in their own way.

People often mistake their most noticeable features for signs that they're not pretty or attractive. I don't agree. Our most noticeable features give our face character and make it all the more interesting to look at. Like a work of art!

Make a caricature of yourself and appreciate your unique features.

WORDPLAY ABOUT MY DAY

EXERCISE:

Write about your day, but make it rhyme. It's as easy as that.

WHY:

Coming up with rhymes takes time so it is a good way to review your day in a mindful manner. Go through your day from the moment you woke up until the moment you went to bed.

ABC all about Me

EXERCISE:

We've all had to recite a customized alphabet for an adult at one point or another in our childhood. Time to make one for yourself. I'll help you get started: A is for Annoyed, that's what I am with this challenge.

WHY:

Creating an alphabet about yourself is a great way to explore the many different facets that make up the gem that is you.

EXAMPLE:

'A: is for ARTISTIC
I love to create

'B' is for BELOVED
since I found my mate

'C' is for CUTE
Because I'm very kind

'D' is for DREAMER
with a beautiful mind

etc. etc. etc. Now it's your turn!

'A' is for…

'B' is for…

'C' is for…

'D' is for…

'E' is for…

'F' is for…

'G' is for…

'H' is for…

'I is for…

'J' is for…

'K is for…

'L' is for…

'M' is for…

'N' is for...

'O' is for...

'P' is for...

'Q' is for...

'R is for...

'S' is for...

'T' is for...

'U is for...

'V' is for...

'W' is for...

'X' is for...

'Y' is for...

'Z' is for...

NOW I KNOW MY ABC AND NOW YOU KNOW MORE ABOUT ME

GOOD OR GROSS?

EXERCISE:

What are the weirdest food combinations you've ever tried and what are some you want to try or are afraid to try? Write them all down on the next page and check them off and rate them when you've given them a try.

WHY:

One time I saw someone eating pizza with whipped cream and I never fully recovered. Everybody has at least one weird food or drink combination that they absolutely love and that makes everybody else wrinkle their nose in disgust.

What are yours? And what are some you've heard of?

Sweet combo's   Rating 0-5:

Option 1: .... ★
Option 2: .... ★
Option 3: .... ★
Option 4: .... ★
Option 5: .... ★

MENU

Hearty combo's   Rating 0-5:

Option 1: .... ★
Option 2: .... ★
Option 3: .... ★
Option 4: .... ★
Option 5: .... ★

PARENTING YOURSELF

EXERCISE:

How would you deal with a child like yourself? For this exercise, we would like you to put yourself in your parent's shoes for a while. What type of parent would you have been for yourself? Do you think you are an easy child to bring up?

WHY:

We all like to think of ourselves as the perfect little angel when we were younger, but let's be honest; most of us probably weren't.

Try to imagine what it would like if you had to parent your younger self. What would you do differently? How would you cope?

This exercise is a great way to practice empathy.

It's totally up to you if you want to apologize to your parents after this exercise.

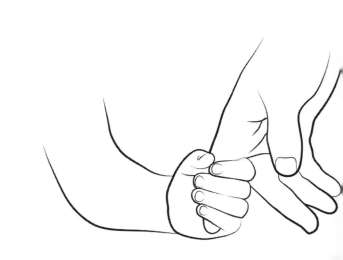

ACROSTIC

EXERCISE:

Do you know what an acrostic is? It is when the first words of each new line in a bit of text form a word. Let's make one for your full name. I can't wait to see what you come up with.

WHY:

I'm not going to lie, it is kind of hard to make acrostics that actually sound good. But that's what makes this such a fun challenge. It challenges you to construct your sentences differently which can drastically change the narrative.

I wonder what you come up with.

EXAMPLE

Let's say your name is Mike. You could make an acrostic like this:

My name is Mike and

i love playing role playing games. I'm a

Knight in service of the Queen. I wish I could play games

every day. But I only play on Friday's.

Please show us that you can do better on the next page.

NAME:

WANDERER

EXERCISE:

Mindfulness is a big deal at the moment and we love it as well.
There are many benefits to centering yourself in the moment and
a good way to practice that is by going for a walk and wandering
aimlessly for a bit. Try it and document the experience.

WHY:

Going for a walk is a great way to practice mindfulness.
Wandering without a goal is a good way to let go. A change of
scenery is also a great way to stimulate your creativity. So when
you feel blocked go outside and take a walk.

I SAW:

I HEARD:

I SMELLED:

I TASTED:

I FELT:

I Saw:

I Heard:

I Smelled:

I Tasted:

I Felt:

I SAW:

I HEARD:

I SMELLED:

I TASTED:

I FELT:

TO DO LIST

EXERCISE:

Make a weirdly specific to-do list for everything you plan to do for the next few hours. Don't leave anything out and be weirdly specific.

WHY:

We all have those days were we feel like we didn't do anything productive. But if you list out all the things you've done you will usually come to the conclusion that you did more than you originally thought.

Think of the next few hours and plan a to do list that is as detailed as possible. You can even include something thoughtless such as 'breathing' on your list.

Are you impressed by all the things you've done? What else could you possibly do in that same time?

TO DO LIST

- [ ] ....
- [ ] ....
- [ ] ....
- [ ] ....
- [ ] ....
- [ ] ....
- [ ] ....
- [ ] ....
- [ ] ....
- [ ] ....
- [ ] ....
- [ ] ....
- [ ] ....
- [ ] ....

TO DO LIST

- [ ] ....
- [ ] ....
- [ ] ....
- [ ] ....
- [ ] ....
- [ ] ....
- [ ] ....
- [ ] ....
- [ ] ....
- [ ] ....
- [ ] ....
- [ ] ....
- [ ] ....

TO DO LIST

- [ ] ....
- [ ] ....
- [ ] ....
- [ ] ....
- [ ] ....
- [ ] ....
- [ ] ....
- [ ] ....
- [ ] ....
- [ ] ....
- [ ] ....
- [ ] ....
- [ ] ....
- [ ] ....

GENIE IN A BOTTLE

EXERCISE:

Oh my God! You're in luck because you've just found a genie in a bottle and you get three wishes! What will you wish for? Keep in mind there are a few rules:

1. No wishing people back from the dead.
2. No wishing for someone to fall madly in love with you.
3. No wishing for more wishes (or for more genies, yeah we're on to you smartypants!)

WHY:

Thinking about this is a great way to learn a bit more about yourself. What are your priorities, what ambitions do you have, what do you need in order to be happy.

Keep in mind though that certain Genie's take great pleasure in messing with your wishes so make sure that you are very clear about your deepest desires.

LIES I TELL YOU!

EXERCISE:

Don't make this a habit but for the next exercise, I want you to lie to me. Describe your appearance but <u>only use lies.</u>

Make a drawing of the person you've described when you're done.

WHY:

Challenge your creativity by coming up with ways to describe yourself that are completely false. It's also a lot of fun to see the person you end up with in the end.

Feel free to ask your friends and family to describe you using a lie as well so that they can be a part of the fun.

I LOOK LiKe...

PORTRaiT

BRUTALLY HONEST TITLES

EXERCISE:

Have you ever heard the original, Hans Christian Anderson version of The Little Mermaid? If so you know that the cutesy title does nothing to prepare young, innocent readers for the brutal ending. Let's give 5 popular fairytales more honest titles.

WHY:

They claim that honesty is the best policy, but it can also put a serious damper on your creativity.

Not in this case though because we are coming up with creative ways to tell the truth about a fairytale without totally destroying people's will to read it.

It would be easy to rename something like 'Beauty and the Beast' into 'Beauty, the Beast and the Bad Case of Stockholm Syndrome', but who would want to read that?

Instead, you can go with: "Beauty, the Beast and the Petty Theft of a Rose"

REAL TITLE: HONEST TITLE:

ZOMBIE APOCALYPSE

EXERCISE:

Are you prepared for the end of the world? No!? What are you doing wasting time then? Let's create a plan for surviving a zombie apocalypse.

You don't want to be caught off guard for that right?

WHY:

Hey, it might happen. There are tons of people who believe that zombies might one day walk the earth so you'd be silly not to prepare for that.

Better safe than sorry right?

THE PLAN

STEP 1:

STEP 2:

STEP 3:

BURN BaBY BURN

EXERCiSe:

OH MY GOSH! The house is on fire and you only have enough time to save three objects. Don't worry about saving your loved ones because your family, friends, and pets are already safely outside. Which material things will you rescue?

WHY:

Family pictures or home video's? That's what most people answer in the first place. They would save something that doesn't have a lot of monetary value but a lot of sentimental value.

What items in your home have the most sentimental value to you and why?

CaN YOU TaMe a DRaGON

EXERCISE:

Imagine this: you were just out for a stroll when you are suddenly face to face with an enormous dragon! This may be your only chance to ever become a dragon rider so tell us how you would go about training your dragon and winning it's trust. Bonus points if you can come up with a cool name for your dragon.

WHY:

This exercise will challenge you to explore your strengths and weaknesses. What about you will make a dragon trust you? What about you will make it want to listen to you?

If you get stuck during this challenge feel free to ask your friends and family to list some qualities of yours.

You'll make this an exercise in confidence as well by doing that. Well, depending on who you ask of course.

POTATO OF POSSIBILITIES

EXERCISE:

Did you think that potatoes are only good for dinner? Think again, there are many ways a potato can be used and we are challenging you to come up with at least 10 unconventional ways to use a potato.

WHY:

Have you ever bought something expensive for a child or a pet only to find out that they are much more into the packaging than the gift itself?

It's amazing how much we can love something seemingly worthless if we just use our imagination. That's what this exercise is for. You can use a potato or any other mundane object you have laying around. Just come up with unconventional ways to have fun with it.

1

2

3

4

5

6

7

8

9

10

HOCUS POCUS

EXERCISE:

Have you ever wished that you could do magic? For this next exercise let's pretend you are actually magic. Come up with a magic spell that is only useful to an extremely niche group of people.

WHY:

It's a good thing magic isn't real. Imagine the trouble we'd be in if that power fell into the wrong hands.

Or even worse, what if that power fell into your hands? What would you do if you had the power to create one magic spell that is guaranteed to succeed.

Would you save the world and solve the climate problems or would you add some zero's to the amount in your bank account?

Your answer reveals a lot about the type of person you are and where your priorities lie. I can't wait to find out.

PURPOSE:

WHEN TO CAST:

INGREDIENTS:

PROCEDURE:

....
....
....
....
....
....
....
....
....
....
....
....

NOTES:

....
....
....
....
....

HOW DO I COMPARE

EXERCISE:

You've probably been told at one point in your life that you have your mothers eyes, your father's nose, or your weird uncles sense of humor. Let's do that again since it was such fun the first time around. For this challenge think of things you have in common with famous people or characters.

WHY:

This is a good way to practice your attention to detail. It may take you some time to find similarities between yourself and famous people or characters, so learn to really look.

This assignment is also perfect if you've ever struggled to maintain eye contact with someone because it feels awkward.

It's also very flattering to realize that you have similar bone structure to a handsome actor or actress.

THIS IS ME

I HAVE THE BODY OF:

I HAVE THE PERSONALITY OF:

I HAVE THE SENSE OF HUMOR OF:

I HAVE THE CHARM OF:

I HAVE THE HAIR OF:

I HAVE THE STYLE OF:

MiNe I TeLL YOU!

EXERCiSe:

Let's pretend that you had the power to claim one invention as your own. The sky is the limit. What would you pick and why?

WHY:

it's crazy to think that everything we use on a daily basis has been thought up by someone else. Whoever thought of swapping banana-leaves for paper has certainly raised the bar for good ideas.

What invention do you admire so much that you wish you'd thought of it yourself?

Try to come up with something that you actually admire for something more than the royalties you'd be entitled to.

DeaD, DeaDeR, DeaDST

EXERCiSe:

is your phone chronically low on battery life or are you an organized person who always charges your phone before you get that annoying low battery warning? Time to put it to the test, return to the next page whenever you think of it and write down the percentage of your phone battery.

WHY:

Honestly, I just want to know that I'm not the only one who will let their phone get all the way down to 2% before charging it.

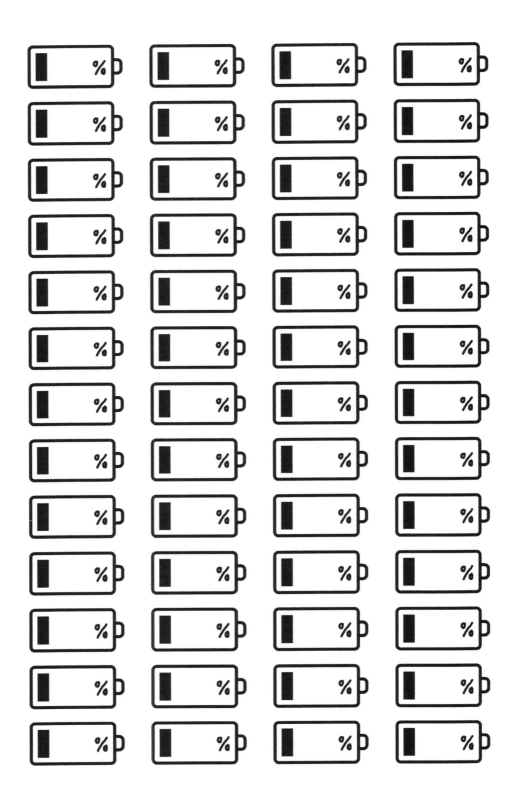

PRANK WARS

EXERCISE:

Have you ever pulled a really good prank on someone? It's one of the best feelings in the world until the realization sinks in that you need to be on your guard for retaliation. Use the next page to plan the perfect prank and make sure to destroy the evidence if things go south.

WHY:

Playing a prank on someone is a great way to ~~get revenge~~ relief stress, make you laugh, strengthen your bond with someone, and promote self-reflection.

It also helps you improve your planning abilities (That last one was just to give you a good excuse).

PRANK

SUBJECT:

REASON:

IDEA:

PREPARATION:

REPORT:

ON MY PHONE

EXERCISE:

What are the most used apps on your phone? How frequently do you use them (or should I say, how much time do you waste on them).

Make a list of all the accomplishments you could have under your belt if you invested your time elsewhere. Does this convince you to change your ways?

WHY:

This exercise promotes self-awareness. Nowadays, everybody has a smartphone. Even on the playground you see little kids with phones. How many time do you spend on your phones and on each specific app?

Fill each square on the next page with the title of an app and the amount of time you spend on it on an average day.

When you add all that time up how much free time are you loosing on your phone each week? What could you do with that time instead?

HOLIDAY CELEBRATIONS

EXERCISE:

Do you love the holidays? Do you think there should be more? Let's come up with a whole new holiday to celebrate. Think of a name, an occasion, traditions, and more to make this the best holiday of the year!

WHY:

Holidays are the perfect time of the year to spend time with family, friends, and loved ones. It's a shame they always need a special occasion. Let's come up with our own reason to celebrate.

NAME YOUR HOLIDAY

DATE   **ON THIS DAY WE CELEBRATE:**

HOW WE CELEBRATE IT...

PROBLEM SOLVER

EXERCISE:

We all know that the world and society is flawed. However with so many people debating over ways to solve the problems in the world one might wonder if a fresh perspective isn't in order. What do you think about the world problems. What obvious solution is staring us right in the face according to you. Use the next page to solve a problem in the world or society.

WHY:

Are you a backseat driver when it comes to politics or social issues? Can you pinpoint exactly what we are doing wrong and how we can do better. Let's hear it then.

Pick a big problem that has a painfully obvious solution (according to you). Extra points if you can solve more than one problem.

THE PROBLEM

THE SOLUTION

FOREVER YOUNG?

EXERCISE:

How old are you now? Thinking back on your life so far, what was the most fun age for you? What made it so great? If you had the chance to be that age forever would you take it? Why? Write about it on the next page.

WHY:

People have always been obsessed with youth. Would you take a sip from the fountain of youth if you were given the opportunity? Or do you welcome old age?

Well too bad, you are sipping from the fountain and you will be this .... age forever!

Why did you choose this age? What was so special about that time in your life? Would you handle your new immortality well?

Bad Habits

EXERCISE:

We've all got habits that aren't particularly good. We know it would be better for us to break those habits, but we simply have no interest in doing that because these habits make life more pleasant or more comfortable. What bad habits do you have no intention of breaking?

WHY:

Everybody has them: certain habits that are generally frowned upon. Habits are hard to break and even harder to get rid of completely.

But, what about the bad habits that actually serve you. Have you been feeling guilty for procrastinating a lot? Maybe you need it for your mental health?

What bad habits are serving you?

HaBiT 1

♥ BeCaUSe

♥ BeCaUSe

HaBiT 2

HaBiT 3

♥ BeCaUSe

♥ BeCaUSe

HaBiT 4

FaSHiON BaBY

EXERCiSE:

Are you easily influenced by fashion? What would you wear if you didn't have to worry about being judged by other people? If you had complete freedom and loads of confidence. Draw or describe your dream-outfit on the next page.

WHY:

There is only one thing standing in the way of you wearing whatever the 'BLEEP' you want and that is your own confidence. Let's pretend for a minute that nobody is judging you. You can be 100% sure of that. What would you wear if you didn't have to worry about the way other people perceive you?

Isn't that a liberating thought? Draw your dream outfit on the mannequin on the next page and tell us why you chose it.

MY STYLE

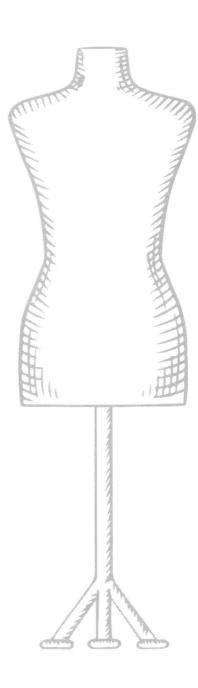

MY TiTLE

EXERCiSE:

Do you enjoy fantasy or royal drama's and do you love those long, elaborate titles that people come up with? Let's come up with a lengthy title for ourselves.

WHY:

Because it sounds prestegious. And also... why not?

INTRODUCING

PiXeL PeRFeCT

EXERCiSe:

Use the next page to make a simple, pixel-art doodle of anything you can think of.

WHY:

Have you ever been intimidated by the art-skills of other journal enthusiasts? When you check social media you'll find millions and millions of aesthetic journal pages by insanely talented people.

Intimidation is a very effective way to block creativity. But, anybody can do pixel-art. All you need to do is color in the different squares to make something cool. You can even use Pinterest for inspiration.

Don't forget to share your creation with us.

RECURRING DREAMS

EXERCISE:

Describe or draw a dream that you have very often. What do you think it means, and why do you suppose it keeps coming back? Freewrite your thoughts or unleash your artistic talent on the next page to capture your dream.

WHY:

We all know that dreams help us cope with experiences from our life. If you've got pent up issues you're likely to be confronted with them in your dreams sooner or later.

Sometimes dreams even help us process things we didn't even know we were struggling with. These dreams tend to come back over and over again until we've dealt with the issue.

What dream do you have very often? What do you think it means. Use your creativity to interpret your dream and don't worry about getting it wrong. We are not basing important life decisions on your opinion at this point.

MY DREAM

MY INTERPRETATION

MY DREAM

MY INTERPRETATION

MY DREAM

MY INTERPRETATION

POOR DESCRIPTIONS

EXERCISE:

Do you enjoy movies, tv, books, or games? Then you'll love this next exercise. Describe your favorite show, movie or story, but do it very badly. Have a look at the examples at the bottom of the page for inspiration. Can you guess which movies we are talking about?

WHY:

Because it is funny. We don't have to be so serious all the time right?

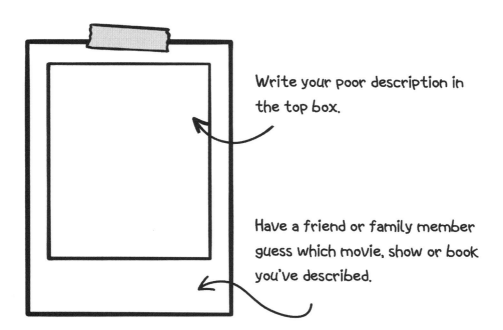

Write your poor description in the top box.

Have a friend or family member guess which movie, show or book you've described.

POOR DESCRIPTIONS

RaNT

EXERCISE:

It's time to unleash the beast. If there is something festering inside of you. A little annoyance that has been building and building without relief, this is your chance. The next page is left blank for one purpose and one purpose only. Rant. Let it all out and don't hold back. Feel free to get aggressive with this particular page if needed.

WHY:

Sometimes you just need to let it out.

Ranting is a great way to relief stress and ranting on paper is one of the healthiest ways to do it.

You can say anything that you can think of without having to worry about what this book will think of you. You're free to let it all out.

Doesn't that feel better?

READY. SET. GO!!!

KEEP GOING...

WOAH, THERE'S MORE?

WHaT iF

EXERCiSE:

We all have 'what if' moments. Moments that could have drastically changed the course of our life if we had just made a different move or decision. Think back to one of your 'what if' moments and rewrite that moment. What do you think would have happened if you had done something differently?

WHY:

There is always that one moment in your past that you keep returning to thinking: "What if".

Sometimes we are haunted by this moment to the extent that we question every decision we've made since then. So if you write an alternate ending for that moment you can finally stop wondering. Decide that that is what would've happened and then write down why you prefer your life the way it is right now.

It's called shadow work, dear. Keep the tissues and comfort snacks close by because you may need them.

ADULTiNG

EXERCiSe:

When you were little, what did you think it would be like to be an adult? Write about how you imagined your adult life when you were just a kid. Have you realized some of those dreams, or have you turned out to be completely different?

WHY:

Your life has probably turned out very different from what you imagined as a child. Let's compare the difference and write a letter to your younger self explaining why you changed your mind about certain things. I'm sure your young self will understand.

ROBOT REVOLUTION

EXERCISE:

What are your least favorite household chores? Let's design a robot to make your life a little bit easier. What type of robot would you build? What would it do and how would it be an asset to your home?

WHY:

Whether you are a chronic procrastinator or if you simply struggle to perform specific tasks around the house there are always certain things we wish we could saddle someone else with.

Let's design a robot made specifically to make your life easier. What should it be able to do. What responsibilities should it take on in your place?

And what would you do with the time that robot frees up for you?

MY ROBOT BLUEPRINT

TYPICALLY YOU

EXERCISE:

Ask your friends and family what they consider to be typically you. Does it match the way you see yourself?

WHY:

Everybody has certain characteristics that are uniquely 'them'. You may have based your entire personality around a fandom, you may be obsessed with a color to the extent that you don't own anything in another shade, and you may have a frog collection that is overtaking your entire house!

What do people associate with you? What makes them think of you immediately? What is typically you?

HOW PEOPLE SEE ME

THIS IS ME

I Love Me

EXERCISE:

Have you ever received a love letter? How did it make you feel? Was it from someone you liked as well or did you have to break a heart? I hope you were gentle.

Well today you are writing a love letter to the person you will spend dthe rest of your life with: yourself.

WHY:

It's important to say nice things to yourself. We already have that inner critic nagging us all the time. Let's shut it up with some words of kindness to give your self-esteem a little boost.

DATE: ..../.........../...........

Dear me,

SUPERME!

EXERCISE:

When did you last feel like a badass? We all have certain role models. People that we look up to because we aspire to be like them. These can be actual people or fictional characters. All that matters is that something about them inspires you to be the best version of yourself.

Make a list of your own personality traits that make you a good role model.

WHY:

It's easy to lose yourself in your admiration of your role model or idol. That is why this exercise forces you to look at your own qualities. Things that make you the type of person that deserves to be admired.

Be kind and generous to yourself and believe in your words.

I'M SUPER BECAUSE

1.

2.

3.

4.

5.

6.

7.

8.

9.

10.

IT TAKES SOME CONVINCING

EXERCISE:

What is your hobby? Your passion? Do you think you could successfully convince another person to give your hobby a try? Well, this is your chance. On the next page write a brief explanation why your hobby is the best thing ever and why everybody should give it a try.

WHY:

Talking about something you are truly passionate about gives you such a rush of dopamine that you'll have a big smile on your face for the rest of the day.

I'm sure that there is a topic that you can give a whole presentation about without hardly any preparation. Well, there is nobody to interrupt you now. Let's hear it then.

THIS IRKS ME

EXERCISE:

Are you a sensitive person? If so you are not going to like this final exercise. On the next page, you're going to make a list of all the sounds, textures, tastes, and scents that just plain give you the heebie-jeebies.

WHY:

We've already had a lot of exercises in this book that have boosted your confidence. promoted your ability to see things from another perspective, grew your sympathetic abilities, and more. We've done enough personal growth for now.

If none of the earlier prompts rattled you I'm sure this one will.

THIS MAKES ME CRINGE!

Made in United States
Orlando, FL
31 January 2023

29271194R00067